[redacted]

Perry H

of Th

by Jim Eldridge

Illustrated by Roger Langridge

Chapter 1

Murder! thought Perry Homes. "Mr Henderson has been murdered!" he said out loud.

Perry Homes and his friend Micky Moxon were in the school yard leaning against a wall. It was break time. Perry turned and looked at Micky to see what he was doing.

Micky was picking his nose. Micky was wondering where all the black bits in his nose came from. Did he breathe them in from the air or were they bits of his brain falling down? In which case, was his brain falling apart bit by bit?

Perry jogged Micky, just as Micky was putting his finger up his nose again. "Ow!" said Micky. Micky turned to look at Perry.

"That could have been dangerous," said Micky. "I might have got my finger stuck up my nose. They'd have to take me to hospital and operate to get my finger out."

"A serious crime has been committed in this school," said Perry.

"What crime?" asked Micky.

"Our headteacher, Mr Henderson, has been murdered!"

Our headteacher, Mr Henderson, has been murdered!

Chapter 2

Micky frowned. Micky was thinking, which wasn't something he did very often. "How do you work that out?" he asked.

"Do you remember what Mr Potts told us yesterday in assembly?" Perry asked Micky.

"No," said Micky.

"Mr Potts told us that Mr Henderson was away on a course," said Perry.

"Oh, that bit," said Micky. "Yes, I remember that bit."

"But do we believe it?" asked Perry.

"Yes," said Micky.

"No we don't!" said Perry.

"Why not?" asked Micky.

"Because teachers go on courses so they can pass exams and get better jobs. Being headteacher's the best job Henderson can get, so it doesn't make sense for him to go on a course. No, it is obvious to me what's happened ... he's been murdered!"

Micky frowned even harder. "Who'd want to murder Mr Henderson?"

"That's what we have to find out," said Perry. "First, we have to make a list of suspects. Then we go to the police."

Perry took his maths book out of his bag and wrote "Suspects" on one of the pages. Then he started to make a list of names.

As soon as school finished, Perry and Micky headed for the local police station. Micky looked unhappy.

"I don't think this is a good idea," he said.

"Why not?" asked Perry.

"Because the police think you're an idiot," said Micky. "You're always coming here reporting crimes that never happened."

"No I am not," said Perry.

"Yes you are," said Micky. "What about those two men you reported last week? You said they were going to rob a bank."

"I heard them say they were going to do a bank job," said Perry.

"They were talking about clearing the bank of the canal," said Micky.

"It was a mistake anyone could make," said Perry.

"Then there was the time ..."

"I'm not talking about this with you any more," said Perry. "A serious crime has been committed and we're wasting time."

Perry hurried into the police station. Micky followed him.

"Yes?" said the desk sergeant. Then he saw who it was. He scowled. "Perry Homes!" he said. "I hope you haven't come to waste our time again."

"Certainly not!" said Perry. "I have come to report a serious crime. Our headteacher, Mr Henderson, has been murdered!"

The desk sergeant looked at Perry and Micky, shocked.

"Murdered!" he gasped. "When did this happen? Who did it? Where's the body?"

"We don't know yet," said Perry. "But I have here a list of suspects."

Perry handed his maths book to the desk sergeant. The sergeant looked at the list. There were fifty names on it.

"Our first list was over a thousand names long," said Perry. "It had everyone in the school on it. Except us two, of course. But we thought that was too many. So we cut out all the pupils and that just left the teachers. And the caretaker. And the school cook. My chief suspect is Mrs Binns, the music teacher. That's because in every TV crime programme I've ever seen, someone is murdered with a blunt instrument. Mrs Binns has the best collection of blunt instruments you've ever seen. Drums, recorders, violins, a piano. Every one of them blunt."

The desk sergeant had stopped listening to Perry. He was glaring at him.

"Then there's Mrs Higgs," said Perry. "She's the school cook. You've only got to taste the food at our school to know that she's a poisoner. An obvious suspect."

"Out!" said the desk sergeant. He pointed at the door.

"What?" said Perry.

"Get out!" said the sergeant again. "Otherwise I'll report you to your parents for wasting police time."

"But Mr Henderson has vanished!" said Perry.

"He's on a course," said Micky.

"I suspect that Mr Henderson has been murdered!" said Perry.

"He's on a course," said Micky again. He didn't want the sergeant phoning his mum and reporting him.

"Listen," said the sergeant. "We've got our hands full trying to find these crooks who are printing fake five pound notes, without you two morons coming in with this stupid story. So get out. Both of you." They got out.

When they were outside in the street, Perry glared at Micky.

"You weren't much help," he said.

“I didn’t want to get into trouble,” said Micky.

“Well, there’s only one answer,” said Perry.

“We go home and forget about it,” said Micky.

“No,” said Perry. “We solve this crime ourselves. We prove that Mr Henderson has been murdered and we find out who did it. Then that sergeant will look silly!”

Chapter 3

Perry and Micky crept along the alley at the back of a large house. Perry stopped by the back gate.

"Whose house is this?" asked Micky.

"Mr Potts's," said Perry. "The deputy head."

"What are we doing here?" asked Micky.

"We are here to look for clues," said Perry.

"Mr Potts is my chief, number-one suspect in this murder."

"You told the sergeant that Mrs Binns, the music teacher, was the chief suspect," said Micky.

"That was before I thought about it properly," said Perry. "Do you know that in nearly every gangster film I've ever watched, whenever a chief crook is killed it's nearly always his second in command who did it. The motive is obvious, it's so he can take over the gang."

"Mr Henderson isn't a crook," said Micky. "He's a headteacher."

"The principle is still the same," said Perry. He opened the back gate and looked in. Mr Potts's garden was in front of them.

"We'll get caught," said Micky.

"No we won't," said Perry. "I heard Mr Potts say he was taking his family out this evening. It gives us time."

"Time for what?" asked Micky.

"Time to look for the murder weapon," said Perry.

They crept into the garden and shut the gate. Perry looked around the garden. Then he let out a gasp.

Micky looked at where Perry was pointing. In Mr Potts's green lawn was a patch of earth which had been dug over recently. It was six feet long by two feet wide.

"This is even better than finding the murder weapon!" said Perry. "This is where he's buried Mr Henderson's body!"

"Are you sure?" asked Micky.

"Look at it!" said Perry. "In every film I've ever seen, whenever there's a patch of earth dug up like that, with those exact measurements, it means only one thing. There's a body under it."

He headed for the garden shed.

"What are we going to do?" asked Micky.

"We're going to start digging," said Perry.

Chapter 4

Next morning Perry and Micky stood in assembly. Mr Potts was giving the whole school a talk about vandalism.

"Last night, I was the victim of vandalism," he told the school. "I went out for the evening, and when I returned home I found that some vandals had dug up the seed potatoes that I had planted!" Micky looked at Perry. Perry pretended not to notice.

After assembly, Micky said to Perry, "So it wasn't Mr Potts."

"We don't know that for sure," said Perry. "He may have hidden Mr Henderson's body somewhere else. Somewhere in the school, for example."

"No chance," said Micky. "For a start, the caretaker would find it."

Perry looked at Micky, his mouth opening and closing as if a new idea had just hit him.

"Of course!" said Perry. "I should have thought of that before!"

"What?" asked Micky.

"The caretaker!" said Perry. "It's obvious! He and Mr Potts are in this together!"

"Why would the caretaker want to murder Mr Henderson?" asked Micky.

"He didn't," said Perry. "I still think Mr Potts did it, but he had to have help. Mr Webb, the caretaker, is the obvious person!"

"Why?" asked Micky.

"Because Mr Potts can't run this school without him. Mr Webb knows everything that goes on here. I expect Mr Potts has paid Mr Webb a big bribe for his help in getting rid of Mr Henderson."

"So what do we do now?" asked Micky.

"Simple," said Perry. "We follow Mr Webb around until he leads us to the evidence we need. Then we'll catch both of them."

Chapter 5

For the rest of the morning, Perry and Micky followed Mr Webb around the school. First, Mr Webb went to the boiler room. Perry and Micky hid and watched as Mr Webb fiddled with the time clock on the boiler. Then he

fiddled with the thermostat. Then he went out.

"You follow Mr Webb," whispered Perry. "I'm going to check the boiler."

"Why?" asked Micky.

"He may be burning evidence. Possibly they even put Mr Henderson's body in it. That's how they got rid of the bodies in this film I saw."

"OK," said Micky.

Micky went off after Mr Webb. Perry went to the boiler. Mr Webb had done something with the time clock and the thermostat. Maybe Mr Webb was making the boiler run hotter so it would burn the body quicker. Perry reached out and switched the boiler to "OFF". That would stop the evidence from getting burnt. As soon as the boiler had cooled down he would come back and open the boiler and dig around for evidence.

Perry went out of the boiler room and hurried up the stairs. As he got to the top of the stairs he could hear an angry voice. It was Mr Webb, the caretaker.

Perry peered round the corner. Mr Webb was standing talking to Mr Potts. With them was Micky! Micky was looking very unhappy.

"This kid was following me around!" snapped the angry Mr Webb.

"Is that true, Moxon?" demanded Mr Potts.

"No, sir," lied Micky.

Well done, Micky, thought Perry. Keep pretending like that and they won't break you down.

"Then what were you doing?" asked Mr Potts.

Micky frowned. He was trying to think of some excuse. "I don't know, sir," he said at last.

"You don't know?" said Mr Potts.

"I don't like kids following me around," said Mr Webb. "It upsets me. It shouldn't be allowed."

"It isn't allowed," said Mr Potts. "Moxon, you will come and see me in my office at break time. Right now you will go to your class."

"Yes, sir," said Micky. Micky went.

"Thank you," said Mr Webb to Mr Potts. Mr Webb went.

Perry watched as Mr Potts walked off towards his office. Micky was in big trouble.

Chapter 6

"I'm in big trouble," said Micky. It was break time and he and Perry were walking towards Mr Potts's office.

"No you're not," said Perry. "Not while I'm with you. Mr Potts won't murder you with me around. He won't want witnesses."

"I'm not talking about him murdering me," said Micky. "I'm talking about him telling my mum I was following Mr Webb around."

Then Micky realized what Perry had just said. "Why would Mr Potts want to murder me?" he said.

"Because of what you know about him and Mr Webb," said Perry.

"I don't know anything about them," said Micky.

"Not yet," said Perry. "But you were about to discover something. That's why he'll want to shut you up." They had reached Mr Potts's door.

"Are you coming in with me?" asked Micky.

"No," said Perry. "He doesn't want to see me. He'll get suspicious if I go in as well."

"Then how will he know that you're around as a witness? You know, in case he tries to murder me."

"I'll start singing," said Perry. "When he hears me singing out here he'll know I'm here."

"Right," said Micky. He knocked on Mr Potts's door.

"Come in!" called Mr Potts. Micky opened the door and went in. Perry began to

sing. He began to sing "Ten Green Bottles Hanging on a Wall" because it was the only song he knew the words of. It was also a song he could keep on singing for a long time.

Perry had just got to "Nine green bottles" when the door of Mr Potts's office opened and Mr Potts looked out.

"Stop that singing, Homes!" he snapped. "You have a voice like a cat being strangled."

"Yes, sir," said Perry.

"And get away from this door."

"Yes, sir," said Perry.

Mr Potts went back into his office. Perry waited and listened. There were no sounds of Micky being murdered from inside the office. After another minute the door opened and Micky came out.

"What did Mr Potts say?" asked Perry.

"He put me in detention tonight," said Micky. "He also told me not to go anywhere near Mr Webb for the next week."

"Brilliant!" said Perry.

"What's brilliant about it?" said Micky. He was fed up. "I'm in detention!"

"It's brilliant that he told you not to go anywhere near Mr Webb for the next week. That's the proof that Mr Potts is protecting Mr Webb! Which means that Mr Webb is hiding some evidence! All we have to do is find out what it is and we've solved the case!"

"Well I'm not following Mr Webb around anymore," said Micky. "I'll only get in more trouble."

"Don't worry," said Perry. "I'll take over following Mr Webb. You go down to the boiler and see if it's cold yet."

"Why?" asked Micky.

"So we can see if Mr Henderson's body is in it," said Perry.

"I'll get into trouble," said Micky.

"No you won't," said Perry.

Chapter 7

Perry followed Mr Webb as the school caretaker walked around the school. Perry followed him to the art room, where Mr Webb did some sweeping.

Perry followed him to the metalwork room, where Mr Webb mended a plug on a lathe.

Perry followed him to the office, where he loaded the photocopier with fresh paper.

Once Perry lost Mr Webb, but only for a few minutes. He found him again coming up from the boiler house. Mr Webb had Micky by the collar of his coat and was hurrying him along.

Perry hurried after them. Was Mr Webb taking Micky off somewhere quiet to murder him? In which case, Perry would be on hand to step in and save Micky at the last minute.

Perry wondered if he ought to find a weapon to deal with Mr Webb when it came to the show-down? Perry searched in his pockets. He had a key, a coin, and a bit of bubble gum. Not much in the way of a weapon there. Maybe he could chew the gum until it was soft enough, and then blow a bubble at Mr Webb and blind him at the last minute.

In fact Mr Webb dragged Micky to Mr Potts's office. Mr Webb knocked on the door, and Mr Potts came out.

"Mrs Reed told me there was no hot water," Mr Webb said to Mr Potts. "I went down to the boiler room and found it had been turned off. And this boy was fiddling with it."

"You again, Moxon!" said Mr Potts. "Why were you messing about with the boiler?"

"I wasn't," said Micky.

"Then what were you doing in the boiler room?" asked Mr Potts.

Micky thought. His face creased with the effort of thinking.

"I don't know," he said, after a while.

"This boy is an idiot!" said Mr Webb. "He ought to be locked up!"

"Moxon," said Mr Potts. "Come and see me at lunchtime. You are in serious trouble. Now get back to your class."

With that Mr Potts went into his office and shut the door.

"And stay away from that boiler, you idiot kid!" snapped Mr Webb as he stormed off.

Perry wondered if he should carry on following Mr Webb, or if he should go and be sympathetic to Micky. The more he looked at the angry scowl on Micky's face, the more he thought that maybe Micky wouldn't take his sympathy in the right spirit. Perry decided to carry on following Mr Webb.

Chapter 8

For the next hour Perry followed Mr Webb as he went all over the school. In the hall. In and out of the toilets. In the gym. In the science labs. And at no time did Mr Webb do anything suspicious. At one time Perry thought he was about to get a clue. This was when Mr Webb was at the back of the canteen. He went to one of the dustbins, lifted the lid, and threw something in. From where Perry was hiding it looked like a bit of sandwich, but Perry wasn't sure.

As soon as Mr Webb had moved on, Perry hurried over to the dustbin. He lifted up the lid of the dustbin and looked in. There was the remains of a cheese sandwich on top of the mess. A terrible smell came from the rest of the dustbin. It was just the sort of place where a murderer would hide a vital piece of evidence, sure that no one would look inside it.

Perry considered digging inside the dustbin and seeing what might be hidden among the rubbish. Then he decided he would ask Micky to look inside the dustbin later.

Perry looked at his watch. A quarter to twelve. There were only fifteen minutes to go before the bell went for lunch time ... He hoped Mr Webb would do something criminal soon. He didn't like the thought of telling Micky that he'd got into trouble again for no purpose.

Mr Webb headed for the office. Perry sighed gloomily. There were no clues in the office. Perry had looked there earlier. For a start there was nowhere to hide anything. Certainly nothing as big as Mr Henderson's body. And there was nothing in the office that looked even a little bit like a murder weapon. Except maybe the photocopier.

Unless that was how Mr Potts had carried out the murder? Maybe Mr Potts had pushed Mr Henderson into the photocopier and then switched it on. Messy, but effective. Perry had to admit that it was an unlikely theory, but then many murders were committed in an

unlikely way. Like in the film he'd seen recently, where the killer had soaked his victim's trousers in nitrogen and his braces in glycerine. As soon as the victim put on his trousers the two chemicals mixed into nitroglycerine and blew him to bits. After that sort of thing, killing someone with a photocopier seemed ordinary.

Perry crept towards the office. He listened. He heard the sound of the photocopier working. It was Perry's guess that right now Mr Webb was using the photocopier to clean the evidence off the inside of it.

Well, now Perry would catch him red-handed!

Then he'd call in the police and they'd arrest Mr Webb and Mr Potts. They'd open the boiler and find Mr Henderson's body. And Micky wouldn't have to go in detention.

Perry leant against the door of the office and listened. The photocopier was still working, there was the sound of paper going chug chug chug as the photocopier printed out.

Perry carefully opened the door and looked into the office. Mr Webb was standing by the photocopier. Perry's heart sank. There was no blood. Nothing. Just pieces of paper coming out of the photocopier. On the pieces of paper were pictures of five pound notes. Perry frowned. Five pound notes?

Perry let the door handle go and it clicked. The noise made Mr Webb look up. Mr Webb saw Perry standing there, looking at the printed five pound notes. Mr Webb scowled. "You nosy kid!" he snarled. "Well, I'll teach you what happens to nosy kids!"

Perry backed away, but found his back against the wall. Mr Webb kept coming. Now Perry saw that Mr Webb was taking something from the pocket of his overall. It was a large and heavy wrench. Mr Webb snarled and lifted the wrench over his head, and then brought it swinging down towards Perry's head.

Chapter 9

By the time the wrench swung down, Perry wasn't there. Perry was running.

"Come back!" yelled Mr Webb.

Perry decided this was not a good time to do as Mr Webb told him. He had discovered that Mr Webb was the crook who was forging five pound notes!

He looked over his shoulder. Mr Webb was running after him, gaining on him. The heavy wrench was swinging in his hand.

Perry wondered where he should run to. To Mr Potts? No, what if Mr Potts *was* working with Mr Webb? Perry would just be running straight into the clutches of the enemy. Perry had seen that happen in too many films. The hero rushes to someone he thinks he can trust, and that person turns out to be the chief villain.

The same could be true of all the other teachers. He remembered the list of suspects he and Micky had given to the desk sergeant at the police station. Every teacher's name was on that list. Say he was right and all the teachers were in on this fake five pound notes racket. There was no one he could trust!

The only answer was to run all the way to the police station and hope he got there before Mr Webb caught up with him. Surely someone would notice a boy being chased by an angry man with a heavy wrench, and say something?

Perry was nearly at the door to the outside now. He rushed the last few paces to it. He threw himself at the bar to push the door open ... but it stayed shut! The door was locked!

He turned. Mr Webb had stopped running now. Instead, Mr Webb was walking towards him, the wrench gripped firmly in his hand. Mr Webb was smiling. His smile made Perry feel cold with fear.

“Mr Potts told me to lock that door to keep out intruders,” he said. “Isn’t it lucky for me I carry out my orders?” Mr Webb had nearly reached Perry now.

“It’s a pity you had to be so nosy, Homes,” said Mr Webb. He swung the heavy wrench up in the air.

"Stop!" shouted a voice. Perry and Mr Webb both looked round. Mr Henderson, the headteacher, was standing in the corridor.

"What on earth is going on?" Mr Henderson demanded. "Mr Webb, what are you doing with that wrench?"

Chapter 10

Perry was shocked. Had Mr Henderson come back from the dead? Maybe he'd only been held hostage somewhere by Mr Potts, and had managed to escape.

"I'll ask you again, Mr Webb," said Mr Henderson. "What are you doing with that wrench?"

Mr Webb hesitated for a moment. Then he said, "I'm doing this!" And he threw the wrench at Mr Henderson.

Mr Henderson ducked and the heavy wrench hit the glass of the fire alarm on the wall near him. The glass broke. The next second there was the sound of the fire alarm going off.

Mr Webb started to run along the corridor. A classroom door swung open just as Mr Webb was passing it. The door hit Mr Webb smack on the head. Mr Webb dropped to the floor, out cold.

By now all the classroom doors along the corridor had opened and all the kids rushed out into the corridor. The teachers shouted, "Don't run! Don't panic! It's only a practice. Stop stepping on Mr Webb, you lot!"

One of the other teachers, Miss Shaw, rushed up to Mr Henderson. "What on earth is going on, Mr Henderson?" she said. "Why is there a fire drill? No one told me there was going to be one. And why is Mr Webb lying on the floor like that?"

"I haven't the faintest idea what's going on, Miss Shaw," said Mr Henderson. "I've only just come back from a course." Mr Henderson turned and looked at Perry. "Perhaps you could tell us what's going on, Homes," he said.

Chapter 11

A short time later, Perry and Micky were in Mr Henderson's office. Mr Webb had been taken away by the police sergeant. The sergeant had congratulated Perry on his detective work.

"Well done, boy," the sergeant said. "This time I was wrong about you. You caught the crook we've been looking for. Just think, he was working under our noses all this time."

After the sergeant had gone, Mr Henderson and Mr Potts both shook Perry by the hand.

"Good detective work, Homes," said Mr Henderson. "It wasn't just me, sir," said Perry. "I couldn't have done it without the help of Micky Moxon."

Mr Potts shook Micky's hand. "I have to apologise to you, Moxon," he said. "I thought you were causing trouble, but all the time you were following Mr Webb and trying to get evidence against him about his forgery business. Isn't that right?"

"I don't know, sir," said Micky.

Mr Potts laughed. "That's what fooled me," he said. "You played the idiot so well, Moxon. Yet all the time you and Homes knew that Mr Webb was really a crook. You two are a lot cleverer than you pretend to be."

"Thank you, sir," said Perry.

"Good detective work, the pair of you," said Mr Henderson. "Well done."

"Do I still have to do my detention, sir?" asked Micky.

Mr Potts laughed. "What a sense of humour!" he chuckled to Mr Henderson. "Of course not, Moxon. In fact, there is one thing both of you can do for me."

"What's that, sir?" asked Perry.

"As you're such good detectives, perhaps you could find out the identity of the criminals who dug up my potato patch the other night?"

Micky looked at Perry. "We'll get on to it straight away, sir," he said.

Later, as Perry and Micky walked home from school, Micky said, "So Mr Henderson wasn't murdered after all."

Perry gave Micky a knowing look. "Oh no?" he said. "Has Mr Henderson ever shaken your hand before?"

"No," said Micky.

"Exactly," said Perry. "In my expert opinion as a detective, that wasn't the real Mr Henderson."

"It wasn't?" said Micky.

"The same thing happened in a film I saw. I reckon they had the other Henderson cloned after they murdered him. I think this one is a replica!"

"We're not going to try and prove it, are we?" asked Micky, fearfully. Perry shook his head.

"One crime solved a day is enough for me," he said. "Let's go and get some chips."